# The Dance of Samhain

## A novella

*This book contains mature themes and
strong language. If you are below 15 years of age,
we recommend you do not continue reading.*

## Maya Jubb

**Story**FACTORY

www.storyfactory.org.au

First published in 2022
Copyright © Maya Jubb 2022
The moral right of the author has been asserted.

All rights reserved. No part of this publication may be reproduced, published, performed in public or communicated to the public in any form or by any means without prior written permission from Story Factory and the author.

Story Factory
storyfactory.org.au

ABN 71 645 321 582

176 Redfern Street
Redfern, Gadigal Land, NSW 2016 Australia
&
90 George Street
Parramatta, Burramattagal Land, NSW 2150 Australia

ISBN 978-1-922719-69-0

Cover illustration and design by Cassandre Collins
Edited by Debra Oswald and Michael Epis
Typeset by Midland Typesetters
Printed in Australia by IngramSpark

Story Factory acknowledges the Traditional Custodians of the lands on which we work and live. We pay our respects to Elders past, present and future and extend that respect to all Aboriginal and Torres Strait Islander peoples.

Story Factory is a not-for-profit that runs creative writing and storytelling programs for young people aged 7 to 17. Supported by our community of expert educators and volunteer tutors, young people are empowered to create stories of all kinds, which we share and celebrate. Young people develop the skills and confidence to find their voice and shape the future.

To get involved, or to find out more, head to storyfactory.org.au

Year of the Novella is one of Story Factory's most intensive programs. Throughout 2022, a committed group of young writers came to workshops every Wednesday afternoon at our Parramatta centre. They shared their stories and supported each other to write. This novella was written as part of that project.

# About the author

Maya is a 16-year-old author with a passion for writing fantasy. She completed the Year of the Novella program last year, and is honoured to do it again. She can often be seen procrastinating on her latest project, or eating Woolies mud cake.

# The Dance of Samhain

## I

'Don't forget to talk to Alardres while you're out!'

León smiled fondly, letting go of the door handle and glancing at his frantic mother. 'I won't, Mamá, I won't.' He placed the heavy, woven box on the wooden table, wincing slightly when he heard it creak.

Taking his mother by her hand, he lightly kissed her cheek, leading her towards the old chairs surrounding the dining table. She sat down and he smiled, keeping his amber eyes locked on his mother's over the chipped surface.

'Oh, and be safe while you're out, too. Would you mind also picking up some apples from Mylisant? I was thinking about making some taquitos-'

León stared at his mother as she rambled on, eventually pressing a finger to her lips. 'I will, I will. Mamá, it's Samhain.' He gripped her hand once more. 'A time of death, yes, and how sad that is, but it's also a time of re-assessment and acceptance.' He tucked a lock of chocolate-brown hair behind her ear, his grip on her hand loosening. 'I'm finally of age, mamá. I've been waiting for this my whole life.' He dropped to his knees, bowing his head. 'I apologise for the outburst, but I'm no longer a child.' He gazed warmly at her. 'It's sad to let go, especially of the past, but isn't that what Samhain's all about?'

His fingers unravelled from around hers, and he stood at his full height. Now, he just brushed the six-foot mark, much taller than his mother, who was barely five-foot six.

He watched the tears begin to well in her eyes, already expecting this reaction from her.

'Oh, you're so much like your father, sometimes . . .' She placed her hands in her lap, smiling sadly up at him.

'I know, I know. You've told me many times before.'

'He was a great man.' He watched the tears become more prominent. 'I'm sure he's so proud of the man you've come today, mijo.'

León brushed the tears away from her slightly reddened cheeks. He didn't respond, already used to her tangents. Every Samhain she would remind him of his father, and that he would 'never truly be gone'. He would catch her staring at the shrine, where the paintings of their family sat.

He couldn't blame his mother for her misery. He had known his father up until he was six, until he tragically passed away. His mother had never explained just what happened to his father; he was able to find out through the townsfolk.

'A nasty illness, the poor guy.' His friend, Taito, had told him. 'Dad says they never knew just what it was. Never seen it before, apparently. Went pale as a sheet, mumbled things no one could make out, coughed up blood. His neck went black too, ash black. Freaky shit, man. They still don't know what it was.'

Never seen before in Valares. Though, not many things happened in their sleepy town, anyway. With little communication with the world beyond the forest, León wouldn't be surprised if the disease was a common occurrence. It was common knowledge by now that the Elders were too stubborn to accept outside help. Perhaps it was pride, perhaps it was a lack of trust, León wasn't sure.

All he knew was that his father had died, and the disease that had killed him had never been seen in Valares again.

'You should go now, quickly. Time will get away from us if you linger for much longer.' The aged woman pulled him down to kiss his forehead. 'Stay safe, mijo.'

León simply beamed in response, hanging his head low for a few moments, before rising once more. 'I will, Mamá, I will. I should go.' He squeezed her hand one last time, before turning on his heel, grabbing the box from the table. He opened the front door, gazed lovingly at his teary mother, and left, closing the door behind him.

'What took you so long?'

Taito ran after him, holding his own box. 'Been waiting for you! I didn't want to hover right next to your front door, that would've been weird.'

León turned to look at his friend, raising an eyebrow. 'What do you think? It's Samhain, you know how my mum gets.'

Taito shrugged, dark eyes widening slightly as a group of children came running past, all wearing light, woollen cloaks to protect them from the autumn breeze. He cursed under his breath, before turning to glare at the kids, who had huddled together, staring at him with wide eyes.

'Watch it, some of us are busy. Don't get in the way.'

León nudged him to get him moving along again, smiling apologetically at the kids. Out of the corner of his eye, he saw them take a few steps back, before running off together again, continuing their game of tag.

'What was I about to say? Oh yeah, *okaasan*. Well, I suppose you can't blame her. Her husband is dead, after all.'

León rolled his eyes. 'Never said I blamed her, she has good reason. Poor thing . . . I miss him too, but I didn't know him that well . . .' He felt a hand on his shoulder, and his head shot up to look at Taito, who smiled softly at him. 'He'll always be here.' He poked him in the chest, causing the both of them to laugh.

'You're so stupid, sometimes.' León shook his head. 'Poke me again and you're dead to me.'

'How mean.' Taito sighed dramatically, resting his head against León's shoulder. 'You're so tall now, fuck you.' He snickered. 'I was taller than you when we were kids, what the hell happened?'

'Dunno, maybe it's because everyone in your family's a blacksmith, and you lot are always short and stocky.'

Taito punched him in the shoulder, causing León to hunch over and hold his arm with his free hand. 'Shit, man. What was that for? I just told you the truth. Some girls are into that, anyway.'

'And some girls are into you. Tall, tanned, dark eyes, charming.' Taito cooed, nudging him, and nodding his head towards the village hall. 'Some guys too.'

León nearly tripped over his own feet, which were stuck between trying to double-take and get away as fast as possible. Taito cackled with laughter, making no move to assist his friend in regaining his balance.

'Careful. Figure out how to stand, he's coming this way.'

León stood up straight, eyes widening as he came face to face with the man he had been trying to avoid.

Ramiro reached out to shake Taito's calloused hand, nodding his head towards him. 'Takaonabe, pleasure to see you.'

'Guerraño-san, the pleasure's all mine.' Taito nudged León, who had been distracted staring at Ramiro. Bronzed skin, chocolate brown eyes, black hair that had been tussled by the wind, and that little scar on the corner of his lips that stretched whenever he flashed that infamous smirk.

Before León had even realised it, Ramiro had been shaking his hand too. 'Maciadonado, pleasure to see you, too. I was hoping you would join in with the celebrations this year.'

When León didn't respond, Taito slung an arm around his shoulders, nodding at Ramiro. 'We wouldn't miss it for the world! Finally nineteen! As if we're not going to celebrate.'

'Yes, I quite agree. Samhain begins tonight, as the full moon rises. Though fun as it may be to have little responsibilities and simply gather around the fire with everyone else, now that we are of age, it is our duty to assist in the preparation of our sacred holiday.'

'True that!'

León, still silent, threw a look at Taito, whose expression told him that he didn't process a word of what Ramiro said.

'Well, if you don't mind, I'll be taking these.' Ramiro took the boxes from both Taito and León, nodding once more.

'Candles and crystals . . . good, you can never have too many of those.' Ramiro then peered into León's box curiously. 'Oh! Pumpkins, we always need more pumpkins. Corn, chestnuts, pinecones . . . your mother always took this celebration seriously, as she should. It was a sad day when we lost your father, he was a great man.' Ramiro smiled warmly at León, making his heart skip a beat. 'He's proud of you, now. I'm sure he is. I hope to see you later today for the lighting of the bonfires, cariño.'

And with that, Ramiro was gone, walking back to the village hall.

'Look at that! He picked up those boxes as if they were nothing, show off.' Taito sighed, looking over at León. 'He didn't even say goodbye to me, either!' He slung his arm over León's shoulders, guiding him away from the village hall. 'He even speaks like he's so much older than us. Isn't he like, only a few months older than you?'

Taito raised an eyebrow as he looked up at León, beginning to chuckle at the far-off expression on his face. 'I really don't know what you see in him, but whatever.'

He let go, beginning to run towards the centre of the village square, gesturing for León to follow. 'Let's go, come on! Busy, busy day! This is going to be the best Samhain ever!'

# II

It turns out that setting up was not as fun as the two boys thought.

León found himself hunched over, hands on his knees and thankful for the cool breeze running through his black hair. Jolts of pain shot through his torso with each strained breath he took, trying to remember the breathing exercises he was taught long ago while playing with the children of the guard.

'What's your excuse?' León found himself glaring at Taito, who was slumped against the wall behind them. 'You're the blacksmith's kid, you're supposed to be better than this.'

'*My* excuse? I'm the blacksmith's *son*, not the blacksmith.'

León rolled his eyes as he straightened his posture, feeling waves of fresh air fill his lungs. Instead of seeing the newly decorated town square, he was now face to face with the cold eyes of the aspiring head of the Valares Guard, Atlas Váromi.

'Now, what do you two think you're doing?'

It didn't feel like a question.

'We're sorry, sir- we just n-needed a break-'

'A break?' His voice was rough and deep from the years of silence he swore himself to.

León could remember years back, when he watched Atlas cry, slumped in the dirt of the training yard. But, they left him there to bleed and fix himself up. He was only six, and León hadn't heard him speak for years after.

Only recently had his voice been put to use again, but only to whisper commands that were so quiet, they overpowered everything around them, echoing through the small town, commanding respect from every person who dared listen.

Atlas turned his nose up at the two. 'A break. Now, how long have you been working?' His dark eyes turned to the sun. The light never reflected off them. They were like black holes, absorbing all the innocent light. That was all his eyes were. A swirling darkness. 'An hour. That isn't long at all.' He faced them once more, but León thought it would have been better if he didn't. He looked as if he was grimacing at the corpse of an unfortunate bug, its guts splattered across the combat boots he always wore.

'Would you care to explain how such little work has earned you rest?' His head snapped towards Taito. 'Back straight.' Atlas grabbed the partisan off his back, hitting the dirt with its blackthorne handle.

Taito jumped back, back impossibly straight. It was as if Atlas was a spirit from the stories León was told as a child. When he wanted something, he got it. When he asked for silence, he got it (not that he ever needed to, chatter ceased the moment he was seen patrolling). When he told you to stand straight, your back could rival a ruler.

Taito bowed low, a long string of rushed apologies slipping past his lips. León would have laughed if he wasn't so scared.

'Yes, sir. Sorry, sir. We'll get right back to it, sir-' Taito's voice was cut short, and León stiffened.

Taito's dark eyes (dark enough to compete with Atlas', but holding much more warmth, normally), were now full of fear. They trailed from Atlas' sneering face, down to his extended arm, to the handle of the partisan, finally ending up locked on the blade now pressed against the pale skin of his neck, propping his chin up at an uncomfortable angle to stare Atlas in the eyes.

Like the armour Atlas wore, the blade was nothing like his eyes. It reflected the sunlight in a blinding way, but commanded the same respect Atlas did. Different sides to the same coin, León supposed.

Taito's Adam's apple bobbed. León could see the beads of sweat forming on his forehead.

'Sir-'

'Get up.'

Taito slowly raised, the partisan's blade following after him, still pressed dangerously hard against his pale skin. A bit more force, and León knew that he would be able to see blood.

'Smart move, Takaonabe.'

His arm swung through the air with enough grace to rival a dancer, and suddenly, the partisan had taken its place on his back again. 'Get back to it. Next time, I won't be so forgiving.'

As he pushed past the two, he stopped for just a moment to hiss into León's ear. 'That goes for you too, Maciadonado. You got lucky this time.'

And with that, he was gone.

'I hate that guy.' Taito managed to get out as he finally regained his voice. León didn't need words to say that he agreed.

A bark of laughter was heard behind the two boys, and they wheeled around to stare.

'Hate's a strong word.'

León began to smile, letting himself slump against the wall again.

Taito, however, was not as relieved. He pushed his chest out and huffed, but the sweat still glistening on his forehead was a clear indicator Atlas' threat was still lingered. 'Samiah, don't you dare do that again. Part of the guard or not, the next time you sneak up on me, I'm going to punch you.'

Samiah looked him up and down with amber coloured eyes, and began to smirk. 'I'm quaking.'

Taito made a grab for her, but Samiah side-stepped, and then wrapped a muscular arm around his neck. 'You do this every time!' She laughed, shaking her head, and then released Taito, who grumbled and fixed his hair.

'And she wins every time.' León let out a chuckle of his own. 'And yet he still does it.'

Taito glared up at him. 'You're supposed to be on *my* side.'

'I don't pick sides, I'm stating facts.' Taito made another weak grab at the air, this time at León, but he was too slow. León stepped back, and then beamed at Samiah. 'You've gotten strong as of late.'

'It's inevitable if I want to make it to the top.' Samiah looked in the direction of where Atlas had gone, but he seemed to have disappeared into thin air. He did that often. He hardly ever left a trace. 'I respect him, don't get me wrong. But I'm sick of it. He doesn't protect, he only destroys.'

'You just want the fancy title and respect.' Taito finally stood at his full height, and looked up at Samiah, who flashed a grin.

'Of course I want the respect, I won't lie about that.'

Taito glanced over at her, before lightly punching her in the shoulder. 'I know it's been rough on you.'

Samiah allowed a gentle smile. 'It has been, but it builds character. I don't care how many people tell me I can't do it. I don't care about the misogyny that's trying to stop me. I'm gonna power through, and become the head of the guard.' She slung her arms around the boys' shoulders, and grinned.

'Who cares about that tonight though? We've got shit to do. Let's get this show on the road boys!'

Samiah's smile was like a disease. Once she broke out into that grin, the two boys immediately followed suit.

'Yes ma'am!' They saluted in sync, and the trio walked away from the town square, laughing the entire way.

# III

León had propped himself up against the old, stone fountain in the middle of the village, watching as people began to set up the bonfires. The sun had just ducked under the treeline, the last drops of sunlight creeping away for the night.

He could see his mother chatting away with Samiah, handing out taquitos and other treats for people to enjoy. He could see Atlas patrolling the boundaries, and Taito with his father, both laughing and spreading the positivity people didn't know they needed. León smiled. Taito was a spitting image of his father. The both of them only wanted to see everyone else smile.

León could see everyone, everyone was gathered in the village square. Everyone but Ramiro.

He scanned the crowds once more. Nothing. Ramiro was nowhere to be found. León weighed his options, and let out a soft sigh. It was worrying that he wasn't here, that was for sure. With the bonfires about to be lit, something that everyone in the town was supposed to witness, León knew that he only had one choice, and that was to search.

So, he stood up straight, and pushed through the crowds, a clay mask clutched tight in his hand. He looked down at it for a second, taking a moment to admire the hard work he put into it. Painted a bright white, with colourful, intricate patterns of flowers and other traditional shapes that formed together to make a skull. He felt the flowers he had fastened to the top, and then the feathers that sprung from the edges of the mask. They were bright shades of red and orange, matching the paint. Just looking at the mask reminded him of the torturous process he had pushed himself through. He had gone through dozens of clay masks in an attempt to perfect his vision. He was proud of how it eventually turned out, though. At least it was entertaining to have Taito beside him, cursing the entire time as he made his own oni mask.

León shook his head and chuckled to himself., deciding to look back up, and continue his search for Ramiro. He walked along the dirt paths, the sound of celebration growing more and more faint the further away he got. He let his feet make the decisions, and fate take the reins, destiny leading him through the town he loved.

He danced around small children, who were chasing each other with arms outstretched, occasionally falling to the ground, their breath being knocked out of them. He would have stopped to see if they were okay, but the last time he had, they had jumped up as if nothing had ever happened, a bright grin splitting their face in two. And, much like it always did, the little boy had jumped up, continuing their game.

He saw the last few stragglers make their way to the town centre, women with their young children, men holding large boxes of firewood. One thing that stayed consistent was that every person he passed smiled at him.

He travelled the outskirts of the town, along dirt paths that slowly became overgrown. He hadn't been down these roads in a very long time. Now that he was thinking about it, the only people who regularly came down here were the guards and the Elders.

Finally, he stopped in front of a winding road, with tree roots jutting out from the dirt, darkness covering the ground like a blanket. León froze. He had been down here once before, once. He was only little, and hadn't got very far. His father had run in after him to take a young León and Taito by the hands and lead them back, lecturing them the entire time.

'That leads to the old temple.' León could remember him saying, in that gruff voice that León struggled to remember. 'No one is allowed to go there, apart from the Elders. Don't go back there again, boys.'

But now, staring into what felt like an abyss, León felt a tug in his chest. Could Ramiro really be over there? He had talked about the temple before, his desire to see the interiors one day, to find out if there was a reason other than the sacred nature of the building why they weren't allowed to be in there.

It wouldn't hurt to check. And besides, it wasn't like he'd go inside. He'd just check outside, that was all.

So, he ventured in, paying close attention to his feet to ensure that he didn't trip over a root or fallen branch. He twirled the string of his mask between his fingers, counting the amount of times it would wrap around his thumb, just to ease his anxiety. He could hear the chirping of birds, the whisper of the wind, and a choir, a ghostly choir of temptation, inviting León to come closer and closer.

He stopped when the path widened out, staring in awe at the ancient architecture. The stone had acquired moss over the years, and had lost its colour as a result of the weather. Dozens of statues were positioned outside of the archways that led into darkness. They were the only things that seemed to remain untouched. The Elders must've taken a long time attending to them, León noted.

They were curious things, León had never seen anything like them. Lions, snakes, birds, creatures he could never even name. There were small, sprite-like beings, and bird women that León could identify as harpies. There was a two-headed dog, mid snarl, a creature that resembled a panther of sorts, with a tail that ended in a clawed hand, and then something that looked like . . . a chicken?

He shook his head and turned his head forward to look at the grandest statues of all. Horses that stood at least twice as tall as he was, every detail intricately carved out. León swore that he could see each strand of hair on their manes. There were four of them, two on each side, facing whoever dared approach the sacred site. However, at the foot of each one was another statue, only half the size of León. Although he would have loved to admire them, they had been overcome by nature, covered in moss and foliage.

And then he saw him. Standing in front of the grand, two-storey temple, was Ramiro, gazing upon a timeworn shrine with a fond smile that only just tilted the corners of his lips. He turned at the sound of León's approaching footsteps, his grin only widening.

'Maciadonado, it's a pleasure. What brings you here?'

León froze as he stared, cheeks slowly heating up. 'I was . . . looking for you. They're about to light the bonfires. I was wondering where you went.'

Ramiro nodded. 'Sweet of you. But we have time. Have you ever seen the *Quattuor Equis*?'

León found himself gazing at Ramiro with a sort of wonderful curiosity Taito always teased him for. He couldn't help himself. His back was impossibly straight, and even standing there, he held a kind of grace León had never seen before. He looked like one of the dozens of statues, pristine, ageless, *magical*.

'No, I never have . . .' León managed, before he stared again. It was a gorgeous building, despite being on the path to ruin. He regretted not coming to see it sooner.

'It's beautiful, isn't it? I'm quite fond of it.' Ramiro walked forward, beginning to climb the weathered stairs, and León held a hand out.

'Don't, you're not allowed-'

Ramiro stopped halfway up, and took in a deep breath of the fresh air. 'León, you know the story of Samhain, correct?'

'Of course I do, but you should really get down, if someone sees you, if someone finds out-'

Ramiro kept his eyes on the darkness inside of the temple. It felt neverending.

'I doubt it.'

León froze. What did he mean by that? Did he really think that he would be able to get away with just waltzing into the temple, or did he doubt that León even understood what Samhain was? Did he do something wrong? Was his basket not good enough? Did Ramiro think he was stupid?

He gripped his mask so hard he feared it might break.

'Not many people know the real story, you see. It's saddening, because I think it's quite interesting. Every year, when the border between worlds is thinnest, spirits break through the *vebice*, and will roam among humans for one night.'

'Yes, I know.' León couldn't help his voice from sounding bitter. Everyone in Valares grew up with the story of Samhain. He didn't need it explained to him.

'But, did you know, that once every seventy years, *vebice* is said to shatter completely. Spirits roam for longer than they should, and a brave warrior has to fix it.'

León furrowed his eyebrows and stared at the man that he had crushed on for so many years. 'Ramiro, what?'

'The events that occur happen to please the four *praenuntias*. But last time, oh last time they weren't pleased at all.' Ramiro turned back to León, his eyes wide and an uncharacteristic smile spreading across his face. It was so wide, León feared that it would tear his cheeks open. He slowly raised his arms, as if to show off the temple. 'León, my dear, sweet León, you're so naive. But I believe you'd make the perfect warrior for the *saltare*, naivety will make you even more entertaining. Your father let them down last time, let's hope you don't do the same.'

Ramiro laughed at the sight of León's confused expression.

'You're cute, Maciadonado.' Though, that didn't make León blush like it used to. 'Your father made it so that this had to happen much sooner than it would've, but I'm sure the *praenuntias* will just *love* you.'

Ramiro's grin grew wider than León thought was humanly possible.

'I'll even make it easy on you, I'll let you see the spirits too! Only because I love you so much.' He cooed, and León took a step back, his heart hammering in his chest. He could hear the faint countdown of the townsfolk, eager to light the bonfires to ward the evil spirits off, and guide their loved ones that had passed back home.

'Just another hint for you too, León. Don't let yourself be blinded by your ignorance and belief in faked morality. Don't be scared to be greedy, it's in your nature!'

Suddenly, the darkness of the temple became a bright white, but León was unable to look away from the sadistic grin on Ramiro's face.

'León Maciadonado, welcome. The Dance of Samhain begins.'

And then, the world cracked to the sound of Ramiro's vicious cackling.

# IV

León ran.

He ran, and he ran, and he ran, and he didn't even know that he could *ever* run this far, but if he stopped, just for a second, he felt like his life would be ripped away from him. Now, adrenaline had taken the reins, and he was going to run until he couldn't anymore.

He forced himself to remember a path he didn't know, jumping over tree roots and pushing past hanging branches. He could feel the world breaking at his feet, tumbling into a never-ending pit. He could hear the cackles of Ramiro, which were significantly louder than the whirlwind of screams and laughs behind him.

He wanted to look around, he wanted to quench his morbid curiosity, see for the first time what was let loose every Samhain. But he couldn't, he couldn't risk his life just for that.

He ran out of the path, his heart attacking his rib cage, threatening to break through.

The sound of his footsteps were deafening in what should've been a quiet night, which was now accompanied by laughing, and screaming, and *tearing*. Like the fabric of his entire world was being ripped apart.

And then, he reached the town.

Before a warning could even slip free from his lips, alarmed for the safety of his people, he realised:

There was nobody else here.

Not a soul to be found. And suddenly, León considered going back to Ramiro. A psychopath as he may be, the company would be nicer than the isolation. The fear for everybody else, wondering what happened to them all. Was Taito okay? Was his mother okay? He would have even taken Atlas, and dealt with his constant abuse, over the isolation.

León closed his eyes tight, for no longer than a fragment of a second, trying to strain his ears for a mere snippet of the celebration, but he heard nothing. He couldn't even hear Ramiro anymore, or whatever sick show he was putting on. There was nothing but a deafening silence.

*They're dead*, was all he could think. *They're all gone.*

All he could do was imagine the worst.

Everyone he knew ripped away from him, torn limb from limb, leaving a gruesome display in the town square.

*The town square,* He realised. *They're in the town square.*

He stumbled forward, the dull thud of his boot against the dirt seeming endless in the ghost town. He found himself asking a question he had never asked before.

'If Taito was here, what would he do?' He whispered to himself, so quiet that he could hardly hear it.

'Probably something stupid.'

León had always been the more responsible one out of the two, he had always been the one that made the good choice. But now, he needed Taito's optimism. What did he have to lose?

He continued his trek forward, clinging onto the last bit of hope that his family was okay, that his friends were okay. That's something he had always admired about Taito. His optimism. It was naive, sure, but it was refreshing. And thinking back on it now, maybe he was just as naive. He may as well be naive and hopeful at the same time.

He had made it further into the town, down familiar streets that felt foreign now. He could see the inn, run by his mother's friend, Alardres. It used to act as a second home for him when he was younger. He could remember sitting on the wooden floor, trying to hide from the older woman. He used to have to put his hand over his mouth to silence himself. His giggling always used to give his hiding spot away. All those years ago, though, he was nothing more than a small child, playing a game where his life *wasn't* on the line. But now, his feet were much too big, and they made too much sound, and he kept tripping over his legs, and he was sure his coordination had never been *this* bad.

Standing in the middle of the empty street felt like a death wish, as if he was giving himself up to be killed right there. He slowly raised his painted mask to his face, holding it in place with the fraying rope.

Suddenly, his heart jumped into his throat, and he began to stumble to the side. He could hear something coming. For a split second, he was relieved. There was somebody else here, he wasn't completely alone.

He snapped out of his optimism. He was being ridiculous. If there was something else here, it was dangerous. Very dangerous.

León slowly backed up against the wall of the inn, palms pressed against the cold stone. He prayed to the gods his father used to worship, names that seemed oh so distant, almost as faded as the memories of his father.

What would he say if he saw me like this?

León slowly clenched his fists, ears straining to pick up on the faint sounds of inhumane laughing and heavy footsteps. Footsteps that were approaching him. Rapidly.

He squeezed his eyes shut, his mask wrapping around his face, blocking any fresh air from reaching his lungs. The clay felt much heavier than it did before, weighing him down. He considered ripping it off and making a run for it, though, he didn't think that his body could handle another sprint. That, and he had nowhere to go. To get to the nearest town, he would have to run back through the woods. Not only did he not know the way, but even glancing at those spindly trees felt like they were twisting around him, pulling him apart. Limb by limb.

And then, he saw it.

It was a small little thing. Perhaps if León had glanced over it, or hadn't been so on edge about everything around him, he would have assumed it was a dog. It was roughly the same size, and, if he hadn't been paralysed in fear, eyes locked on the creature, he would have said it walked the same way as a dog, too. But, it *didn't*.

With every step, its long legs cracked, bending at unnatural angles, bones sticking out of elastic skin. He could see each bone, too thin to support the creature's weight, threatening to snap each time it moved.

It stopped, and so did León's heart.

And then, ever so slowly, it turned its head in León's direction.

Similarly to the rest of its body, the skin was wrapped around its bones so tightly that it may as well have not been there at all. Jagged teeth ripped through the jaw, sticking out at odd angles, ripping through the remaining skin.

Its eyes were the worst part.

Maybe it was because the creature was staring right at him, but León swore that even if he wasn't in this situation, those eyes would have stuck with him until his dying days. If he didn't know any better, León would have assumed that there weren't any eyes at all. They were so empty, so *dead*.

He waited for it to attack, unable to even look away. All he could do was stare at his fate in its lifeless eyes.

And then, it turned away.

It just- *left*. It simply went back to stalking the ghost town, rounding a corner and disappearing.

He sucked in a shaky breath, and slumped against the inn wall. He could still feel his heart pounding against his chest, and his head's relentless attack on itself.

And then, someone had grabbed him, a grip so strong on his wrist that he feared it would shatter. He tried to scream, but before he could even get a sound out, a familiar, rough voice hissed to him, 'shut *up*, Maciadonado. You'll kill us all.'

He turned to face the lane he had been pulled into, and in the shadows, he was immediately greeted with a large boar mask, with two sets of wickedly sharp tusks that curled up to the dark sky. Past the shaggy fur, León saw two figures standing behind the man who had grabbed him.

To his left, was a woman with an elongated wooden mask, carved with sharp lines that trailed up the snout, towards the eyes, and then up the long ears. The lines seemed to have been originally painted, but the red had long since faded.

There was a man standing on the other side of the boar, who slumped against the wall, staring at León with shadowed eyes. The mask was a bright red, with a grin that quite literally stretched from ear to ear. Large fangs jutted out from the mouth, and two black horns extruded from the forehead.

León peered into the depths of the eyeholes, shadowed by the heavy eyebrows of the mask. He began to grin, a feeling of relief washing over him. He *wasn't* alone. He recognised the mask, that much was true, but he didn't *need* to recognise it. Those eyes were familiar enough as it was.

'Taito.' He whispered, and the man looked up.

'León.' Taito whispered back, standing up off of the wall, and taking off his mask to smile at León. 'I was worried about you, man.'

# V

León couldn't help himself from jumping forwards at the sight of his best friend. Maybe it was adrenaline, or maybe it was his absolute relief to not be alone in whatever mess he was now involved in.

'I've been so worried about you.' León whispered, clinging on to the thick fabric of Taito's kimono. 'I didn't know where anyone was- I thought I lost *everything*-'

'Reel it in, ladies.' The hyena grabbed León by his shoulder, pulling him back.

'*Samiah?*'

'In the flesh.' She raised the mask, revealing dark eyes. But, the usual glint of mischief seemed long gone, replaced by masked worry.

'You two are okay.' León wiped his eyes on his bare arm, beaming at his two friends. 'What about everyone else? Are they all safe? Is my mother okay?'

'Your mother's fine, Maciadonado.'

León turned towards the gruff voice, the one that he only now recognised. Not many people called him by his last name, and he knew no one in the village who spoke so quietly, but still so powerfully. The man reached up to his boar mask, lifting it over his head. Underneath was Atlas Varomi, looking as determined as ever.

'And so is everyone else. But, if we don't figure this out, they won't be.' Atlas put his mask back on, and then clicked at Taito and Samiah, both of whom scrambled to do the same. 'Follow my lead, got that?' As Leon placed his own mask back on his face, Samiah scoffed.

'Who made *you* the leader?'

Atlas looked out of the passage, checking the deserted streets. 'If you were good enough to be the head of the guard, then you'd be the leader instead.' With that, he walked onto the street, beckoning the trio with one finger. Despite reluctance from all three, they obeyed.

'He's so full of himself.' León heard Taito mumble from beneath his mask.

'You, front. Now.' Atlas pointed to his side. Before León could process that Atlas was talking to him, Taito had pushed him forward. He stumbled, taking a quick moment to eye the partisan on the man's back. He quickly ran forward to take his spot, deciding that he didn't want to be on the other side of that blade this time.

'I consulted the old history books a couple of years ago.' Atlas spoke. 'They discuss events similar to what we are experiencing now. The *saltare*, it's described as. Latin for 'dance'. Spirits don't return to Inferis, and the gates instead have to be sealed by four warriors, one to take on each *praenuntia*. Though, I couldn't find much on how exactly they do that, or who the *praenuntias* even *are* . . .'

*Praenuntias* . . . León could recall Ramiro mentioning the word, too, but he hadn't expanded on it very much. In fact, it seemed like all Ramiro did was describe unfinished stories, a puzzle with a missing centre.

'I had no idea you knew so much about this,' Leon said.

'Of course you didn't. It was easier for you to believe that I was nothing more than a cruel, power-hungry sociopath, willing to do anything to reach the top.'

All went silent again, the weight of Atlas' words roaring through the streets like a tsunami.

León found himself constantly checking over his shoulder, ensuring that the dog from before, or god forbid, something worse, wasn't following them.

'It's not back. Yet, that is. It might be.' Samiah finally assured him, though León had his suspicions that it was to simply break the awkward silence.

'It didn't attack me before-'

'It's all in the masks.' Taito tapped his own mask. 'They think you're one of them. Stupid things they are.'

Atlas quickly shushed him. 'Don't get cocky. The next

thing you know, we're down to three, because you're being skinned alive by those things-'

'Yeah, like some sort of human sacrifice.' Samiah teased, punching Taito in the arm, who promptly stepped away from her to avoid another assault.

'A sacrifice?' Atlas suddenly stopped, his voice clearer than León had ever heard before. 'Yes, yes that's *it*. The old temple. It could help-'

'*No.*'

Everyone stopped, and turned to look at León.

'No?' Atlas inquired, his voice dropping back down to normal. 'Might I ask, what do you mean, *no*?'

'I . . . I just . . .' he looked towards the other two for support, but they seemed clueless, and, even though it hurt him to admit it, *suspicious*. 'The temple *is* sacred, after all . . . we really shouldn't go in there-'

'León.' Taito stopped him. He had never seen his friend so serious before. A wave of guilt washed over León. 'Where were you when the bonfires were lit?'

It should've been a simple question. He could've just told them that he was there looking for Ramiro, making sure he was safe. And he could've told them that Ramiro turned out to be a psychopath, willing to help open the gates of Inferis. He had information, information that could help him, and his friends, and even the town. There was no point in *not* telling them.

'I suppose I really processed everything tonight. It all got so overwhelming, I couldn't stop thinking about my dad. And, well, I just needed some time to breathe, time away from everyone. I didn't expect to be gone for as long as I was.'

The lie had left his lips before he even noticed.

Atlas crossed his arms, and León tried to keep eye contact. He was thankful for the mask covering most of his face. Atlas was a professional at reading faces and picking apart lies. León just hoped he had an advantage by being mostly covered.

'Then why were you so far away from the town square? In fact, it looked like you were walking *away* from the forest.'

'I wasn't really paying attention to where I was going-'

'Stop tearing into the poor guy- his dad *died*, Atlas,' Taito interjected, stepping in front of León, to prevent Atlas from continuing his interrogation. However, when León nodded towards Taito in an attempt to thank him for his help, all his friend did was turn his back to him completely and continue on their trek. Even Samiah hardly gave him a passing glance as she followed.

After what felt like an eternity of silence to León, they reached the road leading to the town square. The guilt encapsulating his heart loosened its hold for a moment, giving way to hope. His mother was okay, and so was everyone else. He could hear them, all laughing and celebrating, belting songs in countless languages, blasting music.

They rounded the corner, and León's eyes (which were used to the dark streets by now), were hit with bright colours, beautiful shades of orange and red, the light of the large bonfires creeping across the ground, fading only a few metres from his feet. He scanned the crowd, immediately relieved to see the familiar figure of his mother, who was now standing with Taito's father. The local children ran around their legs, still continuing their game.

They didn't know. They had no idea. *Everything* had changed. But his people stayed the same. The town stayed the same..

'We told you they were okay,' Samiah whispered from beside him.

Just as León was about to lift his mask to wipe his eyes, Atlas gripped his wrist again. 'Don't, ' was all he whispered.

León would have tried to rip his arm away, but he knew that he would end up with a broken bone if he did. Before he could question Atlas' sudden panic, he had reached out a hand, gesturing for León to look past the bonfires.

All that previous hope was short lived.

Behind the crowd of townsfolk, behind the light from the fires, there were hundreds of creatures. Dogs like the ones he had seen before, creatures that looked almost human, but with leathery skin, and arms replaced by featherless wings.

'These masks are the only thing keeping us safe from those spirits. I can't stress this enough, León, but we *do not* take these off. Not unless you have a death wish.'

León nodded slowly, letting his hand drop. He watched a jaguar prowl along the outskirts of the light. Its tail flicked, and suddenly, a hand uncurled from the tip of its tail. The creature reached out for the light. However, the moment its fingertips reached the glow, it hissed, and backed away. The hand was smoking, as if the jaguar had touched the flames themselves.

'That's an ahuizotl.'

He wasn't sure what made him suddenly blurt it out, maybe it was the realisation, or maybe it was the memories of his father speaking of such creatures.

'They can't touch the light.' Samiah whispered, straightening her posture. 'The fires are protective, the town is safe as long as they stay in the light-'

'Brilliant observation. If you knew anything about Samhain, you would've already known that.' Atlas hissed.

Samiah faltered, keeping her eyes on the ground instead. Before León could attempt to comfort her, he saw something out of the corner of his eye.

He watched a shadowy figure step forward, into the light, with no troubles whatsoever. The shadows began to swirl around the figure, before seeping into it, leaving a colourful skeleton underneath. It walked forward, and León's heart jumped into his throat.

The skeleton walked forward a couple of steps, stopping only once he had reached León's mother. Ever so slowly, it reached out an arm, wrapping it around the woman's shoulders.

'Dad...' was all he could whisper.

He took a step, reaching out a hand. But, just as it reached the light, it began to burn. He yelped and pulled it away, covering the now smoking skin with his other hand.

'What the...'

'We can't touch the light either.' Taito took him by the shoulder, and pulled him away. 'Does this mean...'

'We're a link between the spirit world and our world.' Atlas too stepped away from the light.

'How do we fix this, though?' Taito looked at Atlas, who stayed silent. León's heart dropped. Ramiro hadn't said anything about closing up the gates, and if Atlas didn't know...

They had no chance.

'Excuse me.'

León whipped around, staring at the owner of the unfamiliar voice. There stood a woman in a horse skull, with flowing red hair, and a discoloured beige dress, tainted by the dirt floor that it swept.

'You can all see them too?' The woman whispered, her hands behind her back. She towered over the group, taller than even León.

Atlas slowly reached back, wrapping his fingers around the handle of his partisan. 'Who are you?'

'I'm from the next town over; I'm here for the celebration. But it appears we've found ourselves in quite a predicament.'

# VI

The woman stared at the group, waiting for any reaction other than their shock.

However, perhaps the shock would have been better, because a second later, Atlas ripped the partisan from his back, slicing the air, and holding it to the woman's bare neck. Unlike Taito's reaction earlier that day, the woman hummed. Even underneath her mask, León could tell that she was staring at the blade.

'That's no way to greet a guest,' the woman said, reaching up with one hand to slowly push the handle down.

Atlas allowed it to drop, but kept it close, ensuring a quick attack if he needed to.

'I must say, I've heard wonderful things about your quaint little town. Though, if all of you are as hot-headed as this, I believe I've made a mistake coming here.'

'Atlas, put the weapon *down*.' Samiah surged forward, grabbing the handle and tilting the partisan downwards.

'What is wrong with you? There's someone else here who can help us, and you immediately attack her?'

'Yeah!' Taito chimed in. León assumed that he had only interrupted to divert Atlas' anger from Samiah to him. 'Leave the poor woman alone. If she can see the spirits too, she must be *terrified*.'

The woman looked at Taito, and then, painfully slowly, turned her head to look at León. Looking into the depths of the sockets of the skull gave him chills. He wasn't sure what it was about it, but that bone looked too real for his liking.

'Lentia.' She stuck out her hand to Atlas. 'My apologies for startling you before. I'm sure we're all just lost and confused right now. I forgive you for your aggression.'

Atlas, however, simply looked at her offered hand, and then turned away, continuing his observation on the spirits.

'We're not all like that, ma'am,' Samiah quickly interjected. 'I promise. Most of us are respectable members of society, who actually care about others and their experiences.' She shook the woman's hand with much more excitement than she normally would. León figured that Samiah was compensating for not being able to greet her with the dazzling smile she was famous for in Valares.

'I'm Samiah Kuatukeun, I'm also from the guard. The one in the oni mask is Taito, and the feathered sugar skull mask is León. The grump over there is Atlas.' Samiah gestured her head towards the man.

'Thank you, dear.' Lentia nodded. 'You mustn't apologise for his behaviour. He is responsible for himself. Though, it's a pleasure to meet you three.'

The woman turned to him again, and León felt a shiver go up his spine. There was something about Lentia that just radiated power. A much different kind of power to Atlas.

'Lentia, if I may have a word.' Atlas looked over his shoulder at the woman. 'Any information we can get can lead to figuring out how to repair the *vebice*, or, the barrier, and seal up Inferis again. Being from another town, I'm sure you have stories from your town that we haven't even heard before. So please, the floor is yours.'

León heard Samiah scoff from beside him. It was obvious what Atlas was trying to do. Perhaps part of him was interested in getting the information, but the two of them knew that all he really wanted to do was call Lentia on her bluff.

'Oh, well, back home, we share stories of an event that occurs every seventy years. It's quite curious, in my opinion. It speaks of four riders, each one on a horse, who emerge during Samhain. Though I can't quite remember the story off the top of my head . . .' Lentia hummed.

'Four horsemen . . .' Atlas mumbled. 'Yes, yes I believe I *have* heard that before.'

'You're just saying that because she did!' Samiah huffed, crossing her arms. 'You can't accept when somebody knows more than you-'

'No, please. I'm curious now. Let him speak.' Lentia spoke gently, holding up one hand. The move immediately silenced Samiah, who, albeit reluctantly, fell back and nodded.

'They're the *praenuntias*, and they run the *saitare* every seventy years. It makes so much more sense now. Four horsemen, four *praenuntias*, four warriors. That must mean that there is one warrior for each *praenuntia*.'

'I . . . yes. I suppose that that could be correct?' Lentia questioned, seemingly utterly baffled by Atlas' speedy, yet (even if it hurt León to admit it), genius interpretation. 'I must thank you for your assistance, Lentia. That will be all.'

Lentia stared at him. 'I'm sorry, what?'

'What part of that did you not understand? That will be all. The four warriors are already chosen. Though I would be much happier with a better group, this is the best team I have. So, thank you, but you are now redundant.' Atlas answered simply, fastening his partisan back to its rightful place.

'She helped us!' Samiah argued. 'We need all the help that we can get. You know that. We can't just push her away!'

'The books state that there are only four warriors, Kuatukeun.'

'And? Who cares? Those dusty books are so outdated. Our Elders still following them is the reason why we can't progress. Does nobody else see that? They're the reason we've never had a woman as the head of the guard.'

'You're bitter you've never climbed the ranks. You're just not *good* enough to command an entire guard-'

'You misogynistic *asshole*!' Samiah charged forward, and León reached out to grab her arm, holding her back before she could give Atlas the chance to hurt her.

'We're never going to make any progress if you two keep arguing!' Taito interrupted, standing between the two. 'I don't care how much you hate each other, please, we need to get through this. We'll take the extra help from Lentia, and we'll pretend to get along for as long as we need to. Now, what do we know so far?'

'There are four *praenuntias*, and the spirits can't touch the light. So, to fix this, maybe we have to lure them into the fire?' León guessed.

'That . . . that's genius!' Samiah looked at León. 'And if it doesn't work, what could go wrong? Yeah, we might *die*, but that's fine. We'll figure it out.'

'I suppose we could give it a shot,' Atlas agreed, looking at his new makeshift team. 'We don't have much of a choice anymore.'

The other three agreed, unaware of Lentia's uncomfortable silence.

# VII

'We'll take shifts. Taito, you'll be patrolling with me. Samiah, León, you two get some sleep.' Atlas ordered. León was thankful for the opportunity to sleep, but when he drew a breath to thank the man, Atlas scoffed and brushed him off.

'He treats us like we're a bother to him,' Samiah mumbled, sitting down beside León on the damp grass.

León simply nodded in agreement, shrugging off his cloak, and laying it on the ground, creating a makeshift pillow.

'He's always been like that. And, I suppose that a situation like this is just bringing the worst out of everyone.'

'I didn't think Atlas could get much worse,' Samiah whispered, looking up at the sky. They had positioned themselves just in the treeline, on top of one of the small hills to the east of the village. It was the best position they could come up with. It gave them a clear view of the entire town, limiting any "sneak attacks", as Atlas had said.

León looked over his shoulder. At the base of the hill lay the town square, fires burning as bright as they originally were. From here, León could still hear the music and cheering. He could see his mother, now, in a similar mask to his own. León strained his neck, trying to catch another glimpse of his father. However, he was simply greeted by more faces he didn't recognise. Transparent figures surrounding their families, and small little balls of light floating around cheering children.

Before he could think more about it, he was torn out of his thoughts by Samiah. She had tapped his shoulder, and then gestured at Lentia. 'Does she seem off to you?' She whispered.

León reluctantly focused his attention away from the celebrating village, looking towards Lentia. The woman was staring in the direction Taito and Atlas had walked off, and even without seeing her face, León could see how tense she seemed.

Samiah observed Lentia, who was standing a few metres away from her and León. She turned when she felt Samiah's eyes on her, seeming slightly taken aback.

'It seems as if I'm not wanted here,' she eventually said, tilting her head towards the direction that Atlas and Taito had walked off.

'Atlas doesn't trust anyone,' Samiah replied, waving a hand. 'Please, Lentia. Lay down, you need sleep as well. I'm sure all the stress has gotten to you by now.'

The older woman shook her head. 'Thank you, dear, but it's quite alright. You mustn't worry about me. I will explore the area. Perhaps I can find something of use to us. A weakness among the spirits, perhaps, or I could find something for makeshift weapons.'

Lentia smiled, watching Samiah open her mouth to protest once more. 'Save your voice, young one. Get some well deserved rest. Perhaps your friend will trust me more if I prove myself to be a valuable asset to you all.'

Samiah slowly laid back down, along with León, placing her hands behind her head. 'You can try your best, but don't get your hopes up. Atlas doesn't trust anybody. Not even his own people.'

León wasn't quite sure when he fell asleep, but suddenly, he didn't quite have a body.

He was stood in a room that felt vaguely familiar, with warm, cream walls, broken up with colourful mosaics and paintings depicting blurred figures he couldn't quite make out. His eyes scanned the room, landing on a large bed, a singular figure under the bright blankets, completely contrasting with the joy of his environment.

The man looked as though he was a shell of a human being. What used to be clear, warm skin seemed to have turned to nothing but rubber, desperately clinging onto whatever muscle he had left. He stared at the opposite wall with eye bags so heavy one might assume he was the victim of two black eyes. However, under those bags, were beads of light. Even in such a state, the man looked so kind, so determined, it sparked something within León.

He knew this place.

He knew this man.

This was his house.

This was his father.

He attempted to call out, but suddenly, he felt a pressure on his chest, as if someone was attempting to crush his ribs. And then, he may have been imagining it, but he swore he heard something from behind him whisper: "enjoy."

The doors opened, and although León was expecting his mother, he was greeted with a woman dressed in all white. Her tattered dress brushed the floor, and from what León could see, it didn't even look like she had any feet. She simply floated towards her destination.

'Mateo Maciadonado. This is your last chance. You either dance with us, or you die. And I will not make it pretty.'

Her voice wasn't human. It was nothing more than a ghostly echo, draining the life out of everything around her simply to be heard.

'Kill me, then. I'm not taking part in your game. I won't be hurting my people for your own entertainment.' His father spoke calmly, keeping his dark eyes trained on the wall. León didn't have many memories of his father, but he didn't recall him being so composed.

'As you wish.' The woman reached out, and under long sleeves, emerged two pale, bony hands. They wrapped around Mateo's throat, and before León could even react, his father's skin had begun to turn black, ash black creeping across a once healthy man's body. 'You've saved nobody.' The woman whispered. 'The process will simply repeat. Perhaps, next time, for your refusal, we'll bring your son into it.'

'Not León, don't you lay a hand on him.' Mateo gasped for air, staring at the woman.

'Don't worry, I won't. Next time, he'll be taken care of by someone much higher up in the food chain. Instead of Pestilence, how about . . . Death pays him a little visit?'

'He's just a kid- don't put him through that-'

But before Mateo could continue his bargaining, he collapsed against the bed, crippled by a coughing fit, and León was pulled through space and time itself, back to the reality of his situation that he completely despised.

He woke up with a scream, shooting up from his place on the floor, eyes wide, and breathing erratic. He clutched the grass beneath his hands, trying to steady himself with something, *anything*.

He jerked his head to the side, tears building up in his eyes. A burning sensation plagued the back of his throat, and before he knew it, he had ripped his mask off, and spilled his guts all over the floor.

'Shit, what happened?' He heard Taito distantly speak to him, attempting to prop him up. 'Man, you need to talk to us.'

'Keep him up straight.' Atlas commanded from the other side of León.

He could begin to see where he was again, still under the once soothing stars, behind the old inn he used to play in. Taito knelt to his right, holding up upright, and Atlas stood for his left, keeping an eye on him. Blurry shapes became clear, and León noticed that both Samiah and Lentia were gone.

'I-I saw him.' León spluttered out, struggling to even breathe. 'It was my dad. This woman came in, and started talking about the dance- she *killed* him. She said that to pay for his lack of cooperation, they'd go after me in the next-'

'León.' Atlas spoke sternly, kneeling down in front of León. 'Breathe. Who was this woman?'

'Pestilence.' León stared Atlas in the eyes. He had never felt so vulnerable, now without his mask. 'She called herself Pestilence. And she said that Death would pay me a visit-'

'Pestilence, Death . . .' Atlas stood up, beginning to pace. 'I've heard this before, there are two others . . .' he mumbled. 'Pestilence, Death . . .'

'War and Famine.' Taito suddenly whispered. 'The other two are War and Famine. We're dealing with the Four Horsemen of the Apocalypse. They are the *praenuntias*. The *saltare* must've occurred before, right before León's father passed. And it didn't go well, so they just repeated the process.' Taito stood up, looking at Atlas.

'That's what Ramiro said.' León whispered before he could stop himself. 'He said that it was my father's fault the *saltare* needed to occur again so soon.'

Suddenly, everything stopped.

'*Ramiro* said that?' Atlas slowly turned to face León. 'Maciadonado, when was this, and how would Ramiro know? Perhaps . . .' he took a step forward. 'Perhaps you met up with Ramiro before all of this happened, and he had something to do with it. Did you lie to us, León?'

It was deathly silent. Both Taito and Atlas stared, waiting for an answer.

León couldn't bring himself to speak. All he could do was slowly stand, and then nod.

# VIII

'We *trusted* you, León. What is *wrong* with you? You *knew*, you knew *all* along. "Oh, I'm oblivious, guys. Look at me, I'm León Maciadonado, I chose someone who hardly knows I exist over my own best friend"!' Taito mocked, slamming his hands into León's chest. 'What did you think was going to happen? You were going to keep this secret forever? No, oh hell no. What is wrong with you? Can you not get it through your thick skull that no matter how much you suck up to him, he'll never like you back? You knew all along. This could've been over so much quicker. Did it not occur to you that people could die? You didn't care, did you? Of course you didn't. You only care about Ramiro, you scumbag-'

León continued stepping back, trying to avoid Taito's wrath. 'Please, listen to me-'

'I'm your *friend*, I *trusted* you, León, but I guess you didn't feel the same, since you were willing to throw all that away for a man who's more interested in a rock than he is in *you*.' Taito spat, hardly taking a break to breathe in between spurts of anger. 'Though, I bet a rock would be more loyal than you are!'

Atlas ran forward, hooking his arms under Taito's, preventing the man from charging forward and attacking León. 'Taito, calm do-'

'Oh no, don't you start telling me to calm down.' Taito hissed, whirling his head around to look at Atlas instead. 'Do you understand how insufferable you are as well? I'd rather hack off my own foot than willingly spend another second in your vicinity. Go and find a war to die in, or even better yet, a cliff to jump off. I'm tired of being treated like I'm less than human by you all. I'm not just your comedic relief, and I'm certainly not the dumb one. In fact, it seems like I'm the only one here anymore that can use their mind at all. It's either you being too far up your own ass to hear what anyone else has to say, or it's León being stuck in fairy land to understand anything other than 'Ramiro's coming this way'.'

Taito ripped himself free from Atlas, who was too stunned to even keep a hold on him. León could never recall a time that Taito ever got this angry.

'I'm sorry, truly.' León whispered, staring at his outraged childhood friend.

The apology did no good, simply setting Taito off again. 'Oh, you're *sorry*? Yeah, I bet you are. But you know what?

Sorry doesn't fix shit. It doesn't fix the time wasted, or the trauma you've put us through, or the fact that you chose *him* over *us*.'

'Can't you shut up for one moment?' Atlas suddenly boomed. Even then, when he was so fired up, Taito quieted immediately. 'Let *me* tell *you* something. We're all mad at León. Grow *up*. You shouldn't have expected any better. If this is the first time you've ever been betrayed like this, you're going to have to get used to it.' Atlas jabbed a finger into Taito's chest. Even though he was cloaked in so much fabric, he flinched anyway.

'You think this is betrayal? I had an entire village turn on me, the village that I risk my life to protect. I'm shunned every day, for following the fate they forced me into. You know what *I* had to deal with? I was a kid, a *kid*. While everybody else had the privilege of enjoying their life, I was taught from the moment I was born that I was nothing more than a disposable soldier. They beat me until I learnt my place, until I gave up. I mute so I could no longer be a burden. Do you know how hard it is? I never wanted this. I was forced to be cruel and hateful. It was just how the Head of the Guard was supposed to act. And guess what? I played the role, it's all I could do. And how do you all thank me? You fear me. You *despise* me.' Atlas spat, turning to León. 'I know what you say about me, too. For someone who knows what happened to me, you sure do like to pretend like you don't. Does it give you a rush? You like playing the victim, don't you? Maybe you're the real monster out of the two of us.'

Taito walked up, and stood behind Atlas, crossing his arms and staring at León. León didn't think he would ever see the time that his childhood friend would side with the man he hated the most.

'What kind of satisfaction does our pain give you?' Taito snapped, each word acting like another stab wound to León's stomach. 'I feel bad for your mother, imagine having to put up with such a spoiled, attention-seeking bitch like you.'

Before León could apologise again, or defend himself, Samiah came sprinting towards them. Her braided hair was a mess, and even with the mask on, León could tell she was panicking.

'Guys, fuck, help! She's one of *them*!'

'Don't ask León for help.' Taito scoffed. 'He can't be trusted.'

Samiah didn't even get the chance to ask what he was talking about, Lentia came galloping towards the quartet on a beautiful white mare. Except it wasn't Lentia. It couldn't be Lentia. The horse mask had been removed, showing a lifeless, sunken in face, a sadistic grin stretching across dry lips. Her neck was ash black, and her hands, her hands were the exact same ones he had seen in his dream.

'Samiah, you're really not going to play the game?' cooed a ghost of a voice. 'Fine then. I suppose I'll have to make you.'

# IX

Atlas drew his attention from León to Pestilence, wasting no time in drawing the partisan from his back. He pointed it at the woman, who did nothing but laugh. 'You're pathetic. You didn't trust me from the beginning. That gave me hope that maybe this wouldn't be so easy for me. But you didn't even make a plan, just in case I was harmful? I expected better.' She flipped her red hair over her shoulder, and smiled at the group. It should have looked innocent, but it was hard for anything to look innocent on such a skeletal face.

'Taito, you know what to do.' Atlas whispered, and suddenly, Taito went dashing off to the side. Pestilence tugged on the reins of her horse, about to charge towards Taito, who was now huddled over a pile of sticks, Atlas jumped in the way of the horse, holding out the partisan for protection, keeping eye contact with Pestilence.

'You're not going near him,' he whispered.

Pestilence began to smile again, which grew into a grin. 'Oh, that's precious. Is your friend of yours making a bonfire to fight me off? That's cute. If you want to get rid of me, go ahead and try, but only the warrior I'm linked to will be able to harm me and my horse.'

Suddenly, a throwing knife went flying into the horse's front leg. It stumbled back with a whinny. Pestilence attempted to calm her down, all while jerking her head towards Samiah, who still had her arm outstretched.

'Then I'll take you on.' Samiah whispered, slowly moving in front of Taito, and drawing another knife. 'You were going to try and pick me off while we were patrolling together, so that the others didn't catch on. You're a *coward*.' She hissed, throwing the second knife with pinpoint accuracy. It lodged itself in one of the horse's back legs. It whinnied, attempting to move away from the threat, but Pestilence refused to let it, keeping a strong hold on the reins.

'You really don't know how to play the game, do you?' Pestilence shook her head, beginning to smirk again. 'This is for our entertainment, not yours. Call me a coward all you want, girlie, but in the end, who has the power here?"

Samiah didn't respond, keeping her body low, slowly drawing another knife. She kept it close to her side, protecting Taito, who was furiously rubbing a stick and dry bark together. León watched his struggle, and then looked at Atlas, who was slowly inching closer to Samiah. Then, giving nobody else time to react, León and Atlas went darting in separate directions.

Atlas ran towards Samiah, shoving his partisan into her hands. 'While Taito makes the fire, you need to hold her off. This is up to *you*, Samiah—'

León, however, went sprinting towards the treeline, grabbing a handful of sticks from the pile that Taito had built up while on patrol.

'What are you all doing?' Pestilence demanded, but the only person who paid her any mind was Samiah. She clutched the partisan's handle, pointing the blade towards Pestilence.

'We're going to finish this, starting with you,' she hissed.

Pestilence forced her horse to move forward, despite the knives in its legs. Samiah wasted no time in swinging the partisan towards the approaching threat, leaving a deep cut in the horse's chest.

León ran back to Taito, throwing the sticks down onto the ground, and beginning to mimic Taito's actions.

'What do you think you're doing?' Taito whispered to him, never raising his gaze once, more focused on his quest to get a fire going.

'Making a fire. We'll need a big one. Consider this help an apology.' León whispered back,

'I'm not going to owe you *anything* after this.'

'I know.' León whispered. 'I'm still going to owe you. There's nothing right about what I did. I'll be making this up to you all for as long as you allow me to.'

Their conversation fell silent. Now, all León could hear were grunts from Samiah, and the huffs of Pestilence's horse.

Suddenly, Taito saw a spark.

As he and Taito continued, more and more sparks appeared, until suddenly, the wood Taito was using was on fire. He hissed and jumped back, hands beginning to smoke. 'We can't touch the light from it.'

León grabbed one of the sticks, and lit it with the small fire. His hand *burnt*, it was agonising, but he kept holding it, standing up, and then heading over to Samiah. He held out the makeshift torch, and Pestilence quickly backed away.

'You're insane-' she hissed. 'You can't touch it either.'

Samiah ran to the fire, and grabbed another flaming stick to wave at Pestilence. The duo held out the fire towards Pestilence, making her back away. However, with the knives in her horse's legs, it couldn't back away in time. The horse's chest began to go up in flames, letting out panicked whines.

'No- *no*.' Pestilence tried to force her horse away, but León threw the torch onto the ground, right underneath the horse.

She was unable to regain control of her horse, which was struggling to get away from the fire, stomping its hooves each time Pestilence attempted to get her back in control, which, subsequently, forced it back into the fire.

Samiah held out the torch as the horse lurched forward, this time burning its muzzle.

The fire had begun to creep up Pestilence's leg now. León was thankful for the smoke. After hearing the paininduced screams from Pestilence, he wasn't sure he wanted to see the exact details of her being burnt to death.

The fire spread, and spread, and spread, and even through obstructed vision, León could see it had covered their former ally's body, creating a morbidly beautiful scene that looked just like a candle.

'You think you've *won*?' She screeched, looking down at the group with crazed eyes. Even Taito had stood up by now, standing behind León and staring in awe, the reflection of the fire dancing in his eyes.

'This is the beginning- this is *only* the beginning! The others will rip you to shreds, they'll *kill* you- you will have wished I had killed you first after they're done with you!'

Samiah simply held out the makeshift torch again, and the woman let out another scream. 'You cruel, vicious beasts!' She threw a hand out, pointing it at León. He stepped back, hands still smoking after his initial attack. 'You're just like your father- he was a horrible man, too! I should have killed him sooner, I should have killed this entire goddamn town sooner-'

'Wrap it up, woman. We've got things to do.' Samiah hissed, holding out the torch one last time.

And, just like that, Pestilence was engulfed by flames, cursing the quartet the entire way out.

# X

It was hard to do anything but stare at the ash that had once been a spirit, attempting to kill every single one of them.

'Samiah, that was brilliant.' León whispered, before quickly being cut off by Taito.

'Don't listen to him.' Taito took the shocked woman by the shoulder, and steered her attention elsewhere, towards the empty streets.

He began a quiet conversation with Samiah, who nodded, leaning in close to hear his story. León didn't need to use much brain power to figure out that they were now talking about him.

He stared at the ash once more, which was beginning to be whisked away by the autumn wind.

That *thing* ruined his life. And Pestilence was only the beginning. Her and the other *praenuntias* were the reason they were stuck in this situation anyway. They were trying to kill him. They killed his dad. They were the reason Taito would probably never speak to him again.

As he stared at the remnants of the fight, Samiah approached him, standing right beside him. She didn't stare like León did. Instead, she kept her eyes trained on his face.

'Hey.' Samiah's voice was soft, broken down by the fading adrenaline from her face-off with such a terrifying monster. 'How're you holding up? She was kinda the one that off-ed your dad, after all . . .'

'I thought you wouldn't be speaking to me. Taito isn't.'

Samiah looked up at him, and then shrugged. 'You had no reason to lie to us, I'm angry. This could've been so much easier if you had told us, but we can't change the past. We need to stick together for the remainder of the *saltare* to ensure that we defeat all four *praenuntias*. After that is when we decide if we're mad at each other.'

León stared at her for a moment, letting her words linger in the air, still tainted by the now thinning smoke.

'That's . . .' He couldn't find his words. Whether it was from the weight of their situation or that he simply would *never* find an adequate way to thank Samiah for her understanding. Or, perhaps it was the fact that he felt like he could feel something squeezing around his neck, preventing him from breathing, let alone speaking.

All he could do was nod.

The corners of Samiah's mouth twitched, but not in the way it normally did. In the past night, it felt as if everyone had changed. León was utterly disgusted with himself. He would have never considered himself to be so dishonest and naive. He had never seen Taito so easy to anger and emotional, and he had certainly never seen Samiah so exhausted. He had never even seen Atlas this stressed, either.

'We should get going.' Taito finally spoke, looking at the dust, and then Atlas.

'Of course.' Atlas huffed. 'I have no doubt that the spirits will have begun to catch on to our plan. We must move quick, and work on the disposal of the other three *praenuntias*. If we linger any longer, we may be under threat of having to face other spirits.'

'To the temple.' León whispered. Even with his voice being almost inaudible, the other three turned to look at him.

They watched him pick up his mask from the grass, wiping off the dirt that had latched on. He didn't spend long in his attempt to tidy himself up, quickly fastening it back to his face.

The trek to the temple wasn't nearly as easy as it had been the first time.

Originally, León's only issue was that he had simply been reluctant. How he wished that was the only issue now.

This time, the issue was that they weren't alone.

There were spirits *everywhere*. Along the streets, in the tree line, speeding past the group.

Originally Samiah had suggested staying away from the spirits at all costs. It was safer, yes. They may have had the masks to protect them, but there was still a chance they would be found out. Smart idea as it was, it was ultimately impossible to carry out.

It was a beautiful view. León would have been stunned if he wasn't so scared for his own life. Fairies flew past his face, not nearly as pretty as he had heard in old fairy-tales. They were grotesque, with large eyes, stringy hair, and prominent bones.

Then he saw the ahuizotl from earlier, slipping past other spirits, head constantly lowered, looking for something to strike.

Taito sped up his pace, keeping his head down. León couldn't blame him. Even Atlas seemed stressed, trying to push past spirits to get to the forest.

When he finally spotted the path, León pushed ahead, gesturing for the others to follow his lead. He began to jog, the other three quickly running up after him. He kept his eyes ahead, noticing that the density of the spirits had begun to drop. In fact, as they reached the end of the pathway, there seemed to be no other spirits at all.

'Weird.' He heard Samiah whisper behind him.

They approached the temple, and the first thing León noticed was that it didn't look abandoned anymore. In fact, it looked pristine, restored to its former glory.

The statues of the horses remained. However, the one to the far left had crumbled. The statue that stood in front of it, unlike the others of the same size, was now free from its moss prison. It depicted a hyena.

Suddenly, it all clicked.

León looked at Samiah, taking in every intricate detail of her mask. Her hyena mask. 'That's you.' He whispered.

Samiah followed his gaze towards the hyena, and drew in a breath. 'If that's me . . .' her gaze drifted to the other three statues, all of which were still covered. 'Those have to be you. When the *praenuntia* is defeated, their statue crumbles, and the victor of the battle is uncovered.'

'Good observation,' spoke a female voice. It wasn't raspy like Pestilence's was, or welcoming like anyone in Valares. It was cold, constantly calculating. Waiting for the right time to strike.

León held back a sigh, slowly turning along with the rest of the group, to be greeted with two mounted figures. A woman with dark hair, and a void for eyes, black dress decorated with skulls. Real, human skulls. Her blood-red stallion was nowhere near as elegant as she was, already huffing, prepared for a battle.

To her right was a man so thin he was practically a skeleton. Stringy, white hair fell over his shoulders, framing a bony face draped in elastic, grey skin. His horse wasn't much better. It also looked like it hadn't been fed in years. Unlike War, who stood beside him holding a sword, he didn't hold a weapon. Insteadhe held a set of scales.

This time, Samiah dropped to the ground behind the group, in a quest to light another fire for their protection. However, the *praenuntias* also were quick to attack.

War went charging for Atlas, who began to dance around the horse's legs, using his partisan to wound them, following Samiah's original tactic. If the horse couldn't move, it was easier to kill it and its rider.

Famine galloped towards Taito, who, unlike Atlas, had little to no fighting experience. He, instead, darted around the horse to avoid it. As they began their wild game of chase, León could hear him mumbling angrily under his breath. '*Famine*? You gotta be *kidding* me! War, Death, Pestilence, and I got *Famine*? That's the *lamest* one!'

León tried not to crack a smile. It wasn't the time to smile. Although, seeing Taito back to his former self was refreshing.

León rushed over to assist Samiah in lighting the fire. This time, he had gotten the hang of the technique, so it was moving much fasters. A spark, and then a flame.

Samiah was the first to notice that something was different this time. While León had to endure the pain in an attempt to set another stick on fire, Samiah was fine. She lit up another stick, and stared at it.

'I'm okay,' she whispered. León's head shot up to see what she was talking about.

'Holy shit.' He began to laugh. 'You're okay!'

'We're not!' Taito shouted, and Samiah quickly got up.

'I defeated my *praenuntia*, that's why I can touch the fire!' She laughed again, and then hurried over to the fighting men, handing each one a torch. She then went back to León, shaking her head when he tried to create another.

'I've got this. Please. Leave it to me. You need to make sure you're in the right shape to fight Death.'

He stared for a moment, and then nodded, backing away from the fire. He wiped his hands on his pants, and then stared at the fight playing out in front of him.

Both Atlas and Taito were utilising the torches, trying to lead the *praenuntias* towards each other. Samiah darted behind them, and set fire to the ground right behind the horses.

It was an impressive sight to see. León had never seen Samiah and Atlas work together. Adding Taito to the mix? It felt like a privilege just being able to see such a rare event.

By this point, the *praenuntias* stood no chance. León watched the two bump into each other, the flames rising up their horses' legs. The two spirits went up in flames, mimicking the bonfires the people of Valares lit every year in an attempt to protect themselves.

The four watched the gruesome show in absolute silence. The *praenuntias* had turned to ash, just as Pestilence had.

'We did it.' Taito let out a shocked laugh.

'We did it,' Atlas echoed, voice much weaker than it was before. León turned to look at him, heart dropping when he saw the large wound in the man's side.

Samiah let out a soft gasp. 'Atlas . . . what?'

'She got me.' Atlas laughed weakly, before immediately holding his side. 'Ah, shit . . .'

Samiah rushed over, holding a hand to his wound to stop the bleeding. León quickly took off his cloak and hurried over beside her, helping her wrap the cloth around Atlas' wound.

'You know, Samiah,' Atlas whispered, smiling up at the panicking woman, 'you were always like a little sister to me. You're the strongest person I've ever met.'

'He's delirious.' Samiah fastened the cloak around him.

'You were always a better fit for the head of the guard anyway.'

León looked over at the now crumbled statues of War and Famine. He watched the moss begin to creep off of the statues underneath, revealing a boar, and an oni.

León turned to stare at the remaining horse and hidden statue instead. He drew a breath, feeling his heart drop. He was next.

# XI

'Might I say, Maciadonado. You have been quite entertaining.'

León spun around, in every direction he could think of, but he saw nobody. Out of every voice he had heard tonight, this was the scariest. It wasn't ghostly, like Pestilence, or gravelly, like War, or even croaky, like Famine. It was . . . normal.

Completely and utterly normal.

Not too deep, but deep enough. No accent he could pinpoint, but he didn't sound like he was from the area. No rasp, no quirks. Completely normal.

And if León had learnt anything over the course of this sick game, it was that normal meant that something was wrong. Horribly wrong.

'I was sceptical, after your father. Pestilence wanted her revenge so bad after that. He didn't play along properly. But *you*.' An excited giggle reverberated throughout the forest. It was too quiet.

'The lie straight off the bat?' The voice kissed the air. 'I've never seen anything like it. Willing to betray your friends and jeopardise the safety of your entire town simply because you didn't want to tarnish your widdle crush's reputation? How cute.' It mocked.

And then, it started laughing.

León couldn't help but be relieved when it did. Its voice started shifting. From a boy around his age, to an old woman, to a child, down to a baby's wail. And then, it wasn't human at all. Or animal, for that matter. It was unearthly. Like the feeling you get when somebody is watching you, or the dread when you know you've forgotten something. It was a time, an event, a place, but never a voice. No voice sounded the way this did.

A figure stepped out of the temple, standing on top of the worn stairs. Except, he *recognised* the figure.

It was León.

'León, I'm Death. It's a pleasure to make your acquaintance.'

Everyone stopped to stare at the man who had just walked out from the temple.

'Please, come up here. We must talk.'

When León simply stared, the *praenuntia* laughed, and began to walk down the stairs. 'Here, we'll meet halfway. How's that?'

León turned to look at Samiah, who simply nodded.

'Fine,' he whispered, cursing his voice for sounding so weak.

He slowly made his way up the stairs, legs shaking with each step.

'There, there you go. It wasn't so hard, was it?'

León slowly shook his head, staring himself in his eyes.

'Oh, you poor thing. You look terrified. Does this form scare you?'

Silence.

'I suppose it is quite frightening, seeing yourself and knowing what comes next. Either I kill you, or you kill me.'

The figure began to shift, now a skeleton, cloaked in a pale blue robe. A pure white horse walked out from the temple to join its master, standing at the top of the stairs and staring at the group below.

'I was just like you, León. Lost, confused, without guidance.' The skeleton sat on the stairs, looking off into the distance. When it spoke, its jaw didn't move, forever stuck in the same position. 'I had a hard life. I lived in a town just like this. And well, it all became too much.'

Now, León could see a rope hanging from its neck. He shuddered.

'We were all humans just like you. And well . . . after becoming a *praenuntia*.' Death laughed. 'It was weird, really. Nothing much changed. I don't have any guilt over what I've done. Becoming this, it taught me something.' It looked at

León, and even though it couldn't, León swore it smiled at him. 'Humans aren't too different from us. I learnt to give into my greed, live life how I wanted to. Well, whatever life I had left. But, I suppose you've taught me something too. Even after life, we can't live forever.'

León stiffened up when Death looked at him.

'Invite your friends up. I'd like to address all of you.'

Samiah and Taito hoisted Atlas up, helping him climb the stairs to face Death.

The group stared in awe at the skeleton, over twice the size of them.

'I'd like to thank you, each and every one of you. You taught me that I can't live forever. And León, you especially.' Death stared at León, who could feel his legs threatening to buckle. 'You taught me that greed is basic human nature. But, you also taught me that so is selflessness.'

León yelped when Death took his hands in its own skeletal ones, examining the forming burns from handling the fire. 'You did well, kid. Your father would be proud. You finished what he couldn't even start. Congratulations, heroes. You have survived the Dance of Samhain.'

The burns on León's hands began to heal, causing him to gasp softly. 'Oh my god . . .'

'Thank you. This life is not one for me. I have played my part. I have danced to my song.' Death gestured towards the makeshift bonfire. 'End it with me.'

León nodded, slowly walking back down the stairs. He grabbed one of the sticks, and lit it, carrying it back up to Death. His hands smoked, but he couldn't feel anything. He was *okay*.

He stopped in front of Death, who nodded at him. 'Thank you, Maciadonado. Kill me now.'

León nodded back, and held out the torch. The fire spread across Death, who unlike its other *praenuntias*, didn't scream. It didn't try to get away. It sat on the stairs, and burnt to nothing but ash.

The white horse at the top of the stairs knelt, and disappeared, becoming nothing but ash that blew away in the wind.

León heard the final horse statue crumble behind him. They had won.

# XII

'You did so well, cariño.'

León hated that voice.

He hated it like he had never hated anything before.

'Ramiro.' León turned to look down at the man he had once loved. 'How nice of you to join us.'

Ramiro stood at the bottom of the stairs, between the two pairs of now collapsed horse statues, hair tussled by the breeze, and dark eyes full of so many emotions, León could hardly pinpoint one.

'So cold. What did I do wrong?'

'You know exactly what you did.'

'How harsh of you.' Ramiro grinned, holding up his hands . 'Look at you up there! Now that the *praenuntias* are gone, you think you've won? The show's just getting started.'

Out of the darkness of the towering trees, hundreds of spirits emerged. The fairies he had seen before, malnourished horses with manes of seaweed, beautiful foxes with countless tails, tall, skeletal humanoids with goat horns protruding from their heads, large spiders, lions with snakes for tails, large snakes the width of León's torso, and dozens of others. He saw elderly women standing behind Ramiro, heads hung low, a melancholy murmur surrounding them.

The ahuizotl crept along the dirt, standing by Ramiro's side, yellow eyes trained on León.

Atlas, trying to appear unfazed, limped up to León's side, followed by a panicked Samiah, who was simply trying to keep the man standing. Taito walked to León's other side, still holding a torch. But even now, that seemed useless against all these creatures.

'Tell us right now, you bastard.' Taito hissed. 'How do we end this?'

'Why on earth would I tell you that?' Ramiro tilted his head innocently, beginning to walk up the stairs. One by one. Ever so closer. The spirits waited, but stayed ready to strike.

'We'll kill you if you don't.' León held out the dagger that Atlas had given him, the blade glinting in the glow of the fire beside it. 'Let me tell you something. We just killed four divine entities, some of the most powerful ones ever known in Valares. You'll be a piece of cake.'

'But will I be?' Ramiro stopped a few steps away from León. 'You may have overpowered them, but can you overpower yourself? Killing the man you've loved for years. It's not that easy, is it?'

Ramiro held out his arms, inviting León to finish him. 'To end the *saltare*, you need to end the vessel, León. Can you bring yourself to do that? To watch the life drain from my eyes? To hate me enough to kill me?'

Atlas tore his eyes away from the man, focusing on León instead. 'You *can* do it,' he whispered. 'This isn't the man you loved.'

And then, Taito spoke, putting his free hand on León's shoulder. And, for a moment, his friendliness made León forget the situation they were in. 'Kill the fucker. He deserves it after everything he's done.'

'One of us could do it instead,' Samiah offered.

'No.' He finally decided, still staring Ramiro in the eyes. 'I want to be the one that does it.'

'Want?' Ramiro began to laugh. 'That's a character arc if ever I saw one. Good on you, kiddo. Do you want a prize? A speech? You still betrayed all of them, you can *never* make up for that.'

Taito held the fire a bit closer to Ramiro. 'It's not about León right now. It's about *you*, and the atrocities *you* committed. Don't start with a scapegoat.'

'A scapegoat?' Ramiro faked shock. 'I would *never*. I just think that you all need to acknowledge León's betrayal. It's not fair to be playing favourites. What if you knew about what I went through? You know *nothing* about me. You take León's side, little, innocent León's side, and paint me out to be the villain.' Ramiro tutted and shook his head. 'Your little celebration here, it was all I had. Does it not sound tempting to you? Begin the *saltare* and survive it. If you manage that, then you replace a *praenuntia*, and control all of this.' He stretched out a hand towards the waiting spirits. 'I have everything you could all ever want. I have an army, Samiah. Atlas, I have all the strength you could ever imagine. Taito? I fit in, for once in my life, I'm being taken seriously. And León,' he smirked at the shaking boy. The banshees began to hum louder, voices stricken with grief. 'I have immortality.'

Ramiro held out a hand, staring at León. 'If I survive to see the morning sun, I control everything. León, I will bring back your father. I'll set him free. He'll come back to the surface, he'll be with you again.' He eyed the dagger still firm in León's hands. 'If you won't do it for yourself, do it for your poor mother.' His eyes trailed back up to León's. 'Don't you want that? Don't you want your father back?'

Ramiro looked back towards the spirits, all of which were patiently waiting for the next move. 'León, if you let me survive until dawning, I'll give you everything you've ever wanted.'

He looked back, and suddenly, his eyes went wide.

León hadn't even thought about it. One moment, he was standing a step away from Ramiro. The next moment, he was holding the man's shoulder, his other arm outstretched, now covered in blood. His dagger was lodged in Ramiro's stomach.

Ramiro slowly raised his gaze to look at León, face rapidly paling. 'You *didn't*-'

'I did,' was all León answered. Out of all things that had happened over the course of Samhain, this was the scariest. Because as he pulled the dagger out of Ramiro, and watched the blood begin to spill from the wound, he felt no remorse. In fact, he wasn't against the idea of stabbing him again. And again. And *again*.

The promise of his father? What a sick joke.

'We have to end the vessel? Two birds and one stone,' León whispered, staring at Ramiro stumble back.

'You can't be *serious*- that's not- you *can't*-'

León looked down at the dagger in his hands. Beautiful as it was, it was now covered in blood, which had even reached the intricate detailing on the hilt. He felt a pang in his chest, as if he had been the one stabbed.

As the wails of the banshees grew ever louder, Ramiro took one step back, and then two, and then he couldn't stop. As the stairs gave way under him, it was only a matter of time before he misstepped, and tumbled back.

The quartet watched as Ramiro gave one last shout, before hitting the bottom of the stairs. In a blur of blood, his skull cracked, leaving his lifeless body on the stone path.

The ahuizotl rushed forward, leaping over Ramiro's body to charge at León. Taito stepped in front of him, raising the torch, but before the creature could reach them, it began to crumble. León flinched back, observing the ash that used to be the ahuizotl be caught by the wind, and blown away.

'Oh my god.' Samiah whispered.

The creatures dropped in waves, each turning into dust which fell to the dirt, burying its way through the cracks in the ground to get back to Inferis. The cries of the banshees died away, until all that was left was Ramiro's body.

But, even then, that crumbled too. León watched Ramiro's body begin to glow, turning into small balls of light, which floated up, and then disappeared in the light of the now rising sun.

There was silence, complete silence.

Ramiro had been right. It was so much harder to kill someone you knew.

'You did it,' Samiah whispered, staring at León. He wasn't quite sure if it was because she was impressed, or simply didn't want to look at the gruesome sight before them.

Taito dropped the torch, and wrapped an arm around León, letting out a bark of a laugh. 'You did it! We did it!' he cheered.

Atlas took off his mask, revealing his tired, but relieved face. 'We did it,' he whispered, before being pulled in by

Taito. He didn't fight against it, instead, uncharacteristically, wrapping an arm back around Taito, and joining the cheering.

'You're going to hurt him!' Samiah lectured, but Atlas instead pulled her in alongside them. Even León, as shocked as he was, couldn't help but grin, grabbing his friends and holding them close.

# XIII

'I must say, perhaps you all aren't as useless as I had originally thought.' Atlas smirked at Taito, who clicked his tongue.

'Shut up.' But even then, Taito couldn't help but laugh.

Atlas had one arm over Taito's shoulder, and one arm over Samiah's, using the two as support to walk.

'When did you get so friendly?' León asked. 'Did you hit your head during that fight?'

Atlas laughed. A true, genuine laugh, one that reverberated off the sky itself. 'Maybe I did hit my head.'

Leon looked towards the approaching town. 'I suppose trauma to that degree can be a character building experience.'

'And a bonding experience.' Taito chimed in, grinning at his friend. 'I think we all learnt something about each other today.'

'And ourselves.' Samiah added.

'Who would've guessed that innocent León over there would be a compulsive liar?' Taito laughed.

And, even with the guilt in his heart, León smiled at them all. It was hard to be mad at Taito when he was smiling that much, blood dripping from his mouth.

'What *happened* to you all?' shrieked a woman's voice once they made it to the town. The bonfires had just gone out, now that the sun had risen, but León could still feel the warmth. That, or he was just happy to be back.

It was Taito's father who ran forward first, grabbing his son and inspecting his face, taking in every last cut and bruise.

After Taito's father, the rest of the townsfolk crowded around them, their questions drowning out into a sea of worry.

'I have an announcement,' Atlas boomed. León was surprised he could still get his voice to be so loud, with such an injury to his stomach.

Suddenly, everything went quiet. Even in such a frenzy, people followed Atlas' every move.

'I'm stepping down.'

Samiah turned her head to look at her superior, her eyes wide. '*What?*'

Atlas smiled at her, another true smile. It lit up his face, and suddenly, León could see a young child again. Before all the hope had been stomped out of him, before he had been forced to turn into such a harsh man.

León hadn't thought that a smile would ever suit Atlas so well.

'This night has been an eye-opener. When everyone else froze under pressure, when the odds were completely against us, one person pulled us to victory every time. I'm realising that Valares needs someone stronger. This is why I'm making Samiah the new head of the guard.'

There was silence for a moment, the reality of the situation sinking into the town. León couldn't blame them. Up until a couple of hours ago, all Atlas was to him was a man who didn't care for his people, simply seeking control of everyone around him. But all León could see in that dazzling smile was a broken child, wanting to right his wrongs.

Cheering began to spread across the people like a wave, deafening León, and most certainly deafening Samiah, who was being crowded by familiar faces, congratulating her and shaking her hand.

León slowly backed away from the crowd, right into someone's arms. When he turned, it was his mother, whose eyes were wet enough to rival a waterfall. 'León,' she whispered, before squeezing him tight, beginning to cry into his shoulder. 'What happened to you?'

'I'm okay, mamá. I'm okay, I promise. I'll tell you everything in a moment,' he whispered back, wrapping his arms around his mother, feeling tears begin to form. And, as he stood there, listening to the town congratulate a shocked

Samiah, he swore that out of the corner of his eye, he saw a human skeleton, painted in bright shades of reds, oranges, purples and greens. It gave him a thumbs up, and then faded away.

# Author acknowledgements

Here we are again, woah?

I'd like to start this with a quote from Bilal. 'Bilal the country, huh? Let's all stare at Kevin, that's what we do. My cat evades taxes.'

It's so crazy to think that I'm back here again. When I first started the novella program last year, I didn't believe that I could even make it to the end. But now, this is my second book, and I hope I have plenty more to follow. I've made so many new friends this year, people who have supported me and have been patient no matter what.

I should thank Bilal first, who has supported me over the past two years in my writing journey, editing my typos, encouraging me when I needed it the most, and laughing at jokes that really didn't deserve a laugh. He has made Story Factory such a welcoming and comfortable space for everyone involved, and I'm sure I speak for everyone when I say that.

I take that back, because the next person I'm thanking is Kevin. Kevin probably isn't comfortable at Story Factory, since we always bully him, but I'm sure he's fine. Thank you Kevin, for helping all of us with our novellas, and for putting up with us, even when we were being close to unbearable.

Before I thank anyone else from Story Factory, I guess I should thank my parents too, or something like that. Really, thank you so much, Mum and Dad. You two have been patient with me all year, but also strict when you've needed to be. Your support in my writing journey has meant so much to me, and I hope I can continue to share my work with you.

Thank you to Adri, who made sure I didn't give up on my writing, and helped me come up with ideas when I was stuck. Not only this, but you've been there whenever I've needed a shoulder to cry on, or a person to share my new obsession with. I hope this book doesn't disappoint you at all.

Thanks Charmaine, who was always there to laugh with me, and always there to comfort me. You've always been like an older sister to me, and I love you girl, thanks for everything.

Adri wasn't the only one who supported me, thank you to all my other friends who supported me in this journey, especially the ones who made sure I was taking care of myself, even when I was trying to reach deadlines, or when I just wasn't bothered. You mean a lot to me, guys, thank you.

Thanks to the illustrator for my amazing cover, too. I was so happy with it when I saw it, and it helped me to continue my writing, even when I doubted it, just so I could see it as an actual book.

Now, onto the students at Story Factory.

Thank you to Avni and Kai, my friends from last year. Though, I'm quickly revoking that thanks to Avni, because she left us to go to 7/11 (aka America).

I'd also like to thank all my new friends, some of whom I met in the first week, some of whom I met later on. There was Coco, who has been one of my best friends, someone who, from the beginning, I've always been able to laugh with, or rant with. There's also Milo, who (on my end, maybe they hated me) I got along with immediately. And I'd like to thank them for starting the Word War, because that made my competitiveness kick in, and actually inspired me to write.

Thank you Sakshi, even if we weren't close, for talking to me every lesson, and supporting me when we both were stressed about our writing.

Thanks Pious, for always playing along with my jokes, and for always being accepting, and H, who, even if we weren't that close, never failed to put a smile on my face.

I'd also like to thank the entire e-family, which started after I proposed to Pious as a joke over text. Thank you to the e-children, Coco and Avni, for being the best e-children a mother could ask for. And thank you to Milo and H, who just went along with the shenanigans, even when they didn't understand.

Thank you to both Bilal and Kevin as a unit, because your prank war always got us smiling, and a very special non-thank you to Kevin's air pump, which never showed up. Also, thank you to Kibbeh, Bilal's cat, who I'm sure is involved in some kind of supernatural activity, and Kinder, the seagull that was out the front of Story Factory one day, who kept coming back for hot chips.

Thanks to all my friends from last year too, who supported me at the book launch when I was terrified, and who treated me with nothing but kindness all year.

Thank you Nan, for driving me to Story Factory every week, and always being supportive of my writing. And thank you to my uncle, who introduced me to the program in the first place.

Also, thank you to my teachers who were, and still are, supportive of my writing. Thank you to the teachers who read my book from last year after I gave it to them, and a special thank you to Mr Hambly, who tried to read it even with a newborn baby in the house.

Thank you to Mr Wallington, who actually ordered my book from last year, and all my other teachers who I hope get to read this one. Thank you, Ms Lowe, Mr Church, Mr Eastwood, and Ms Gatsios.

And thank you to everyone else I haven't mentioned. This book wouldn't be possible without the endless support and help from those around me. So thank you everyone.

# Acknowledgements
## Story FACTORY

Year of the Novella 2022 was made possible thanks to the support of a group of generous donors:

Bernadette Brennan & Justin Gleeson SC
Rosebrook Foundation
Caroline Beecham & John Lydon
Greg Dean & Richard Unsworth
Kim Anderson
Deena Shiff & James Gill

This publication would not have been possible without the unstinting support of the editorial and production teams at Penguin Random House. In particular, we would like to thank Claire de Medici, Ben Fairclough, Catherine Hill, Kathryn Knight, Melissa Lane, Patrick Mangan, Nikla Martin, Phoebe McKenzie, Shané Oosthuizen,

Jodie Ramodien, Vishali Seshadri and Mary Verney. Extra special thanks to Catherine Hill and Patrick Mangan for managing Penguin Random House's involvement in the project, and always being so supportive and enthusiastic. Thanks also to our freelance editors and all-round fantastic Story Factory volunteers, Michael Epis, Amy Denmeade, Monica Tan, Debra Oswald, Sarah Brandon, Sheridan Jobbins, Philippa Stewart, George Palathingal and Vania Caldas. Finally, massive thanks to our pro-bono typesetters, Midland Typesetters, and the generosity of printer Griffin Press.

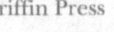

Griffin Press

www.ingramcontent.com/pod-product-compliance
Lightning Source LLC
Chambersburg PA
CBHW011958090526
44590CB00023B/3779